Survival

written by David Orme and Helen Bird
illustrated by Beccy Blake and Jackie Harland

Contents

Introduction

Living in the wild is tough.

There might be lots of food one week, and hardly any the next. The weather is constantly changing. In many parts of the world, extreme conditions bring special survival problems. And there is always the chance that something is lying in wait, ready to eat you! Being eaten is a special problem for plants – they can't run away as animals can.

Animals and plants are under constant pressure, not just to stay alive, but to breed to make sure that their species can survive into the future. Over millions of years, living things have learned to adapt to whatever nature throws at them.

Now nature faces its biggest challenge – the environmental problems caused by man, the most successful **species** of all. But even in the face of this, some animals are fighting back!

In the freezer

The frozen wastes of the Arctic and Antarctic are harsh places to live. Winter temperatures can drop as low as -50 degrees Centigrade, and powerful winds whip up the snow into blizzards.

And yet these parts of the world are full of life. In the Antarctic, colonies of penguins brave the ice and snow. In the Arctic, the polar bear is a feared **predator**. The seas provide food for everyone. On the land, hardy plants have found their own way to survive. Each living thing has found its own special survival techniques.

*The Emperor penguins of the Antarctic huddle together in **colonies** to keep warm.*

Case Study 1

Lichens

You may have seen grey or yellow marks that spread over roofs, tree trunks and old stone walls. These are lichens, one of the world's greatest survivors!

Lichens' special trick is to be two plants in one, an **alga** and a **fungus**. These plants work together in a special way. The alga is able to use sunlight, air and water to make food by **photosynthesis**.

- *The alga and fungus work together to produce food so the lichen can live.*
- *Lichens can survive in very low temperatures.*

The fungus traps water from the air and provides the alga with a framework to grow on. In exchange for this, the alga provides the fungus with food. Lichens are very slow growing, and some are thought to be over 4,000 years old.

In the Arctic, a special form of lichen called reindeer moss can survive at very low temperatures. It is a vital food for reindeer; without it they would be unable to live in this bleak region.

Lichen

Reindeer moss

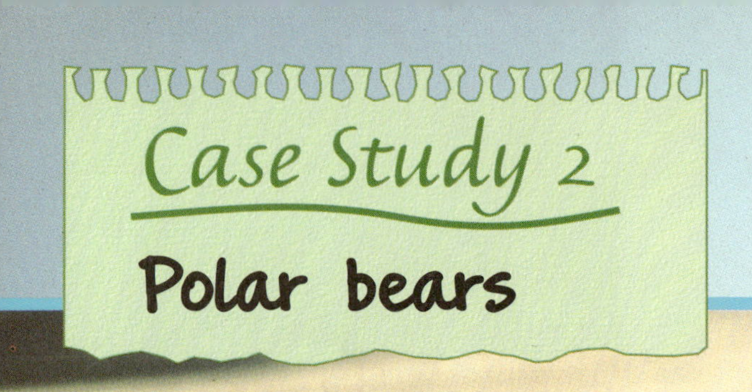

Case Study 2

Polar bears

Polar bears are well adapted for life in very cold places. Their thick fur keeps them **insulated** and warm. They have a strong sense of smell, which means they can scent **prey** from a long way away. Their powerful claws can kill a seal with one blow.

Breeding is difficult for polar bears. The females give birth once every two years. In between they build up their strength and body weight.

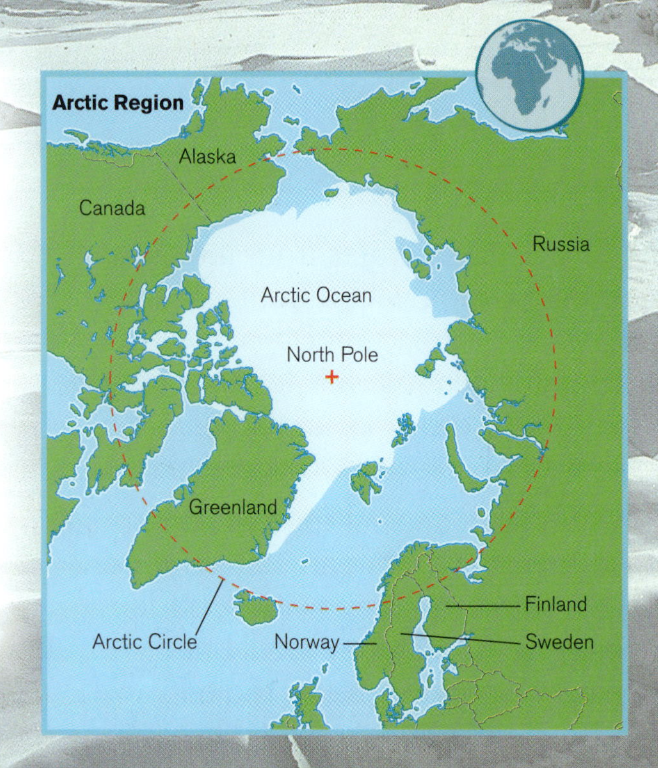

- *Strong sense of smell can locate prey from great distances.*
- *Long, sharp claws to kill their prey.*
- *Thick coat keeps them warm.*

At the end of autumn the female bear builds a **maternity den**. When the cubs are born, they each weigh under one kilogram. They stay with their mother in the den until spring. All this time the mother **suckles** her cubs and lives off her own body fat. They leave the den only when the warmer weather comes. It is another year before the cubs are strong enough to hunt for themselves.

Some like it hot

The world's deserts are another extreme **habitat**. There is little water, and temperatures often reach 50 °C, higher than any animal could survive for long. Yet deserts often have a wide range of plant and animal species.

Lizards move quickly over hot surfaces so that their feet don't burn!

How do they survive?

Many creatures spend the hottest parts of the day in **burrows**. They come out only in the cool of the evening or at night. Some desert lizards have learned to move quickly over hot surfaces, stopping in cooler shady places.

Plants are unable to move, but they grow thick skins and fleshy leaves that don't quickly shrivel in the heat.

Water is a scarce **resource** in the desert, and both animals and plants need to find ways to store water or to use as little as possible.

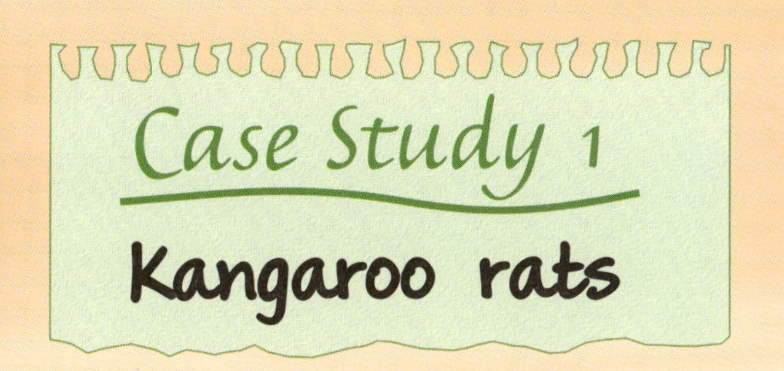

- *Kidneys recycle water.*
- *Nose absorbs moisture.*
- *Creates own water.*

The kangaroo rat is well adapted to survive the harsh desert life. During the day it retreats to the cool of its underground den, where it carefully seals off the entrance with soil. This stops the hot desert air reaching it, and also prevents any precious moisture from its own body escaping into the air.

Kangaroo rats have very specialised **kidneys**. Their kidneys can recycle water from urine so little water is lost from the body. They have developed special noses which can absorb moisture from the air – including any that is breathed out by the rat itself!

Kangaroo rats also have an amazing survival trick. They can create their own water from the hydrogen and oxygen in the driest of foods. In fact, they are so **self sufficient**, that they don't drink water even if they are offered it!

Case Study 2

Barrel cacti

The cactus is affected by the problems faced by desert animals. It has to cope with great heat (and sometimes extreme cold, for deserts can be very cold at night) and shortage of water. It has another problem too – animals see cacti as a source of food and water, and a cactus cannot run away or hide in a burrow!

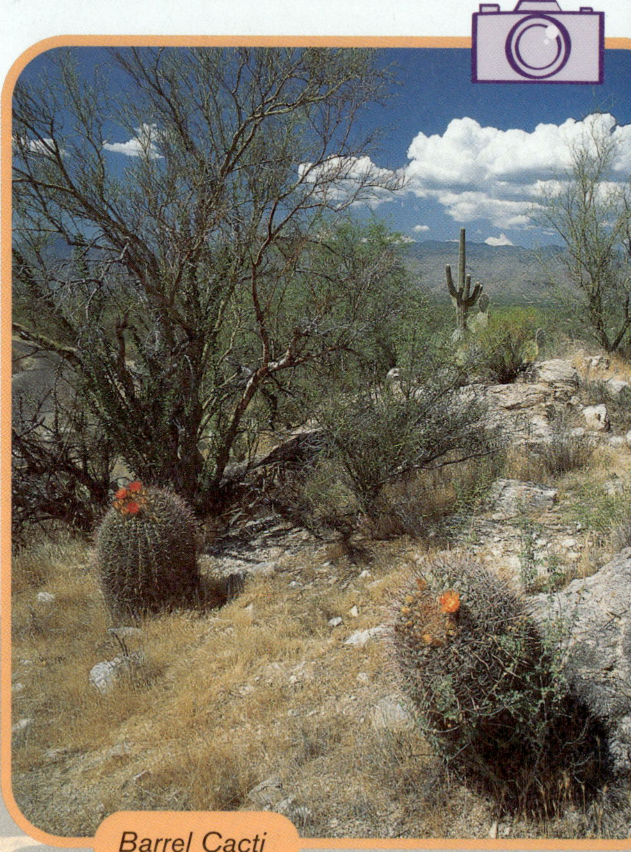

Barrel Cacti

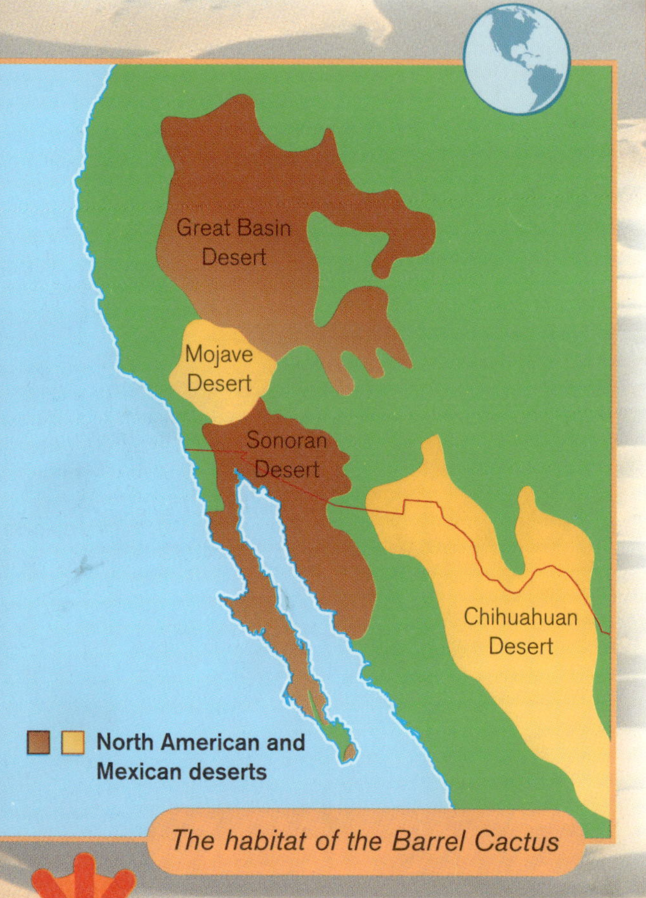

The habitat of the Barrel Cactus

Most plants have leaves, which is where they make their food. But in the desert leaves would soon shrivel; so the barrel cactus has none. It does have extremely long roots which can spread over a wide area to capture as much moisture as possible.

Rain is rare in the desert, so the cactus uses its barrel-shaped body to store large quantities of water when it is available. These plants can survive years of **drought** on the water collected from a single rainfall.

Seeds of all desert plants need to be able to resist drought. Cactus seeds can live for many years, waiting for the rain that will bring them to life.

Everyone knows that cactus plants have spines! The spines put off animals who would want to eat the cactus. They also trap air to make an insulating blanket, protecting the plant from heat and cold.

- *Large roots spread out to collect water.*
- *Barrel-shaped body stores water.*
- *Spikes protect from predators and insulate cactus.*

In the dark

Darkness has its benefits. If you can't be seen it is easier to avoid being eaten! But there are problems, too.

In the dark, how do you move around without bumping into things?

How do you find a mate, or your next meal?

How can plants grow in the dark, when light is essential to the process of making food?

Yet even in the darkest places there is life. In deep caves where no light ever reaches, insects scuttle around looking for food, such as the droppings from bats or birds.

Fish with no eyes swim in dark underground lakes. In the deepest parts of the oceans fish live in a world of total darkness.

Many creatures take advantage of the dark to hunt at night – but to do this they need a few very special tricks.

Case Study 1

Bats

During the day bats hide away in dark places such as caves, the trunks of rotten trees, or in the roofs of buildings. But when evening comes they are ready to start hunting for food.

How do they manage to fly in the dark without bumping into things?

Although bats have small bodies, they have huge ears. As they fly they make very high-pitched squeaks which are too high for most people to hear. The bats listen for the echoes of the squeaks to tell them where things are.

This is rather like a radar (or echo location) system, which was invented in the twentieth century to help boats and aeroplanes find their way. Bats have used their "radar" system for millions of years!

The main problem bats face now is finding suitable places to roost because modern buildings do not have as many dark hiding places as old ones did.

Bats have learned one important rule of survival: do something that other creatures can't do!

- *Huge ears provide very good hearing.*
- *'Radar systems' listen out for prey and prevent them from banging into things in the dark.*

At the bottom of the deepest oceans, it is pitch dark and the **water pressure** is enormous. Yet somehow the fish that live there manage to survive.

In the vast areas of total darkness at the bottom of the sea, you might think it would be hard to find a mate. The male anglerfish can detect a female fish from far away. Once he has found his mate, the male attaches his mouth to her body so he cannot lose her again!

One extraordinary trick that deep sea fish have evolved is to make their own light! This is called '**bioluminescence**'. Light is created by chemical changes in the skin. Using this light, fish can even flash messages to each other!

The anglerfish takes this a stage further. It has a 'fishing rod' jutting out from its head. At the end of this rod there is a light. When a curious fish arrives to see what is going on, the huge jaws of the anglerfish are waiting!

Some bioluminescent fish

- *Fishing rod style light attracts prey.*
- *Good sense of smell detects a mate.*

Not getting eaten

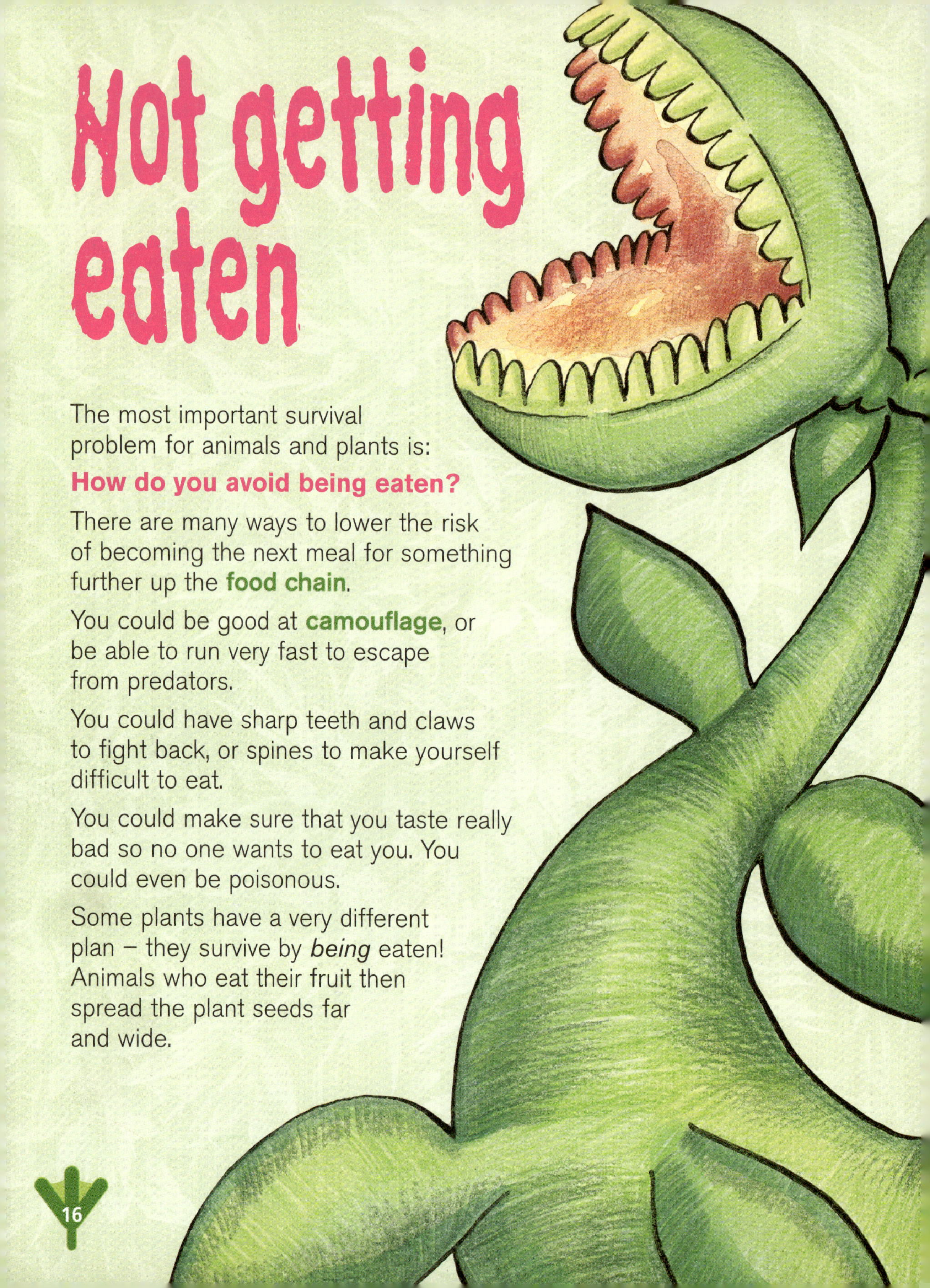

The most important survival problem for animals and plants is:

How do you avoid being eaten?

There are many ways to lower the risk of becoming the next meal for something further up the **food chain**.

You could be good at **camouflage**, or be able to run very fast to escape from predators.

You could have sharp teeth and claws to fight back, or spines to make yourself difficult to eat.

You could make sure that you taste really bad so no one wants to eat you. You could even be poisonous.

Some plants have a very different plan – they survive by *being* eaten! Animals who eat their fruit then spread the plant seeds far and wide.

Case Study 1

Sensitive plants

Many predators like to catch their prey live; they will ignore any dead creatures they may find. Some animals take advantage of this by 'playing dead'. What is surprising is that there are some plants that can do this, too! They are called sensitive plants.

If you touch a sensitive plant the leaves will immediately flop. What appeared to be a succulent leaf now looks dry and withered, not worth eating! If an insect lands on the plant looking for a meal, the collapse of the leaf may even make the insect fall off the plant.

This plant is extremely sensitive to vibration. The faintest touch of a finger will cause them to collapse, and they can detect the vibrations made by a grazing animal's footsteps – or even its breath!

- *Senses vibrations around it and collapses to look dead.*

Case Study 2

Thompson's gazelle

It is a hot day in the Serengeti National Park in East Africa. A herd of Thompson's gazelle is feeding. On the edge of the herd young males are keeping watch for lions, hyenas and cheetahs. The Thompson's gazelle has very good eyesight, vital for survival.

One of the young males has sighted a predator! He shakes and stamps his feet in alarm.

No predator will attack the entire herd. It will try to pick off solitary animals on the edge, and these young males are especially at risk.

Now the predator is ready to attack. The gazelle will have to rely on its speed to avoid being eaten. It can run at 55 kilometres per hour (kph) for up to 15 minutes and can go as fast as 80 kph when running from predators. While it runs it takes great leaps in the air. This leaping, or 'pronking', enables it to see where it is going and to check where the predator is.

Finally the chase is over. This time the predator has its meal – the young male is lost, but the breeding females have been saved.

- *Sharp eyesight spots predators.*
- *Staying close together in a herd gives protection from predators.*
- *Run very fast to escape predators.*
- *Young males sacrifice themselves for the future existence of the species.*

Looking after baby

Survival is important for individual animals and plants, but survival of the whole species is even more important. To make sure the species survives, animals and plants produce **offspring**.

But how can they be sure that the offspring will survive?

Many creatures look after their offspring for months or years, until the young are old enough to look after themselves. But for some living things, such as plants and many sea creatures, looking after their young is impossible. And so another trick is used: producing so many thousands of offspring that at least a few are bound to survive.

Alternatively you could just let your young be reared by someone else!

Most turtles produce up to 200 eggs at a time.

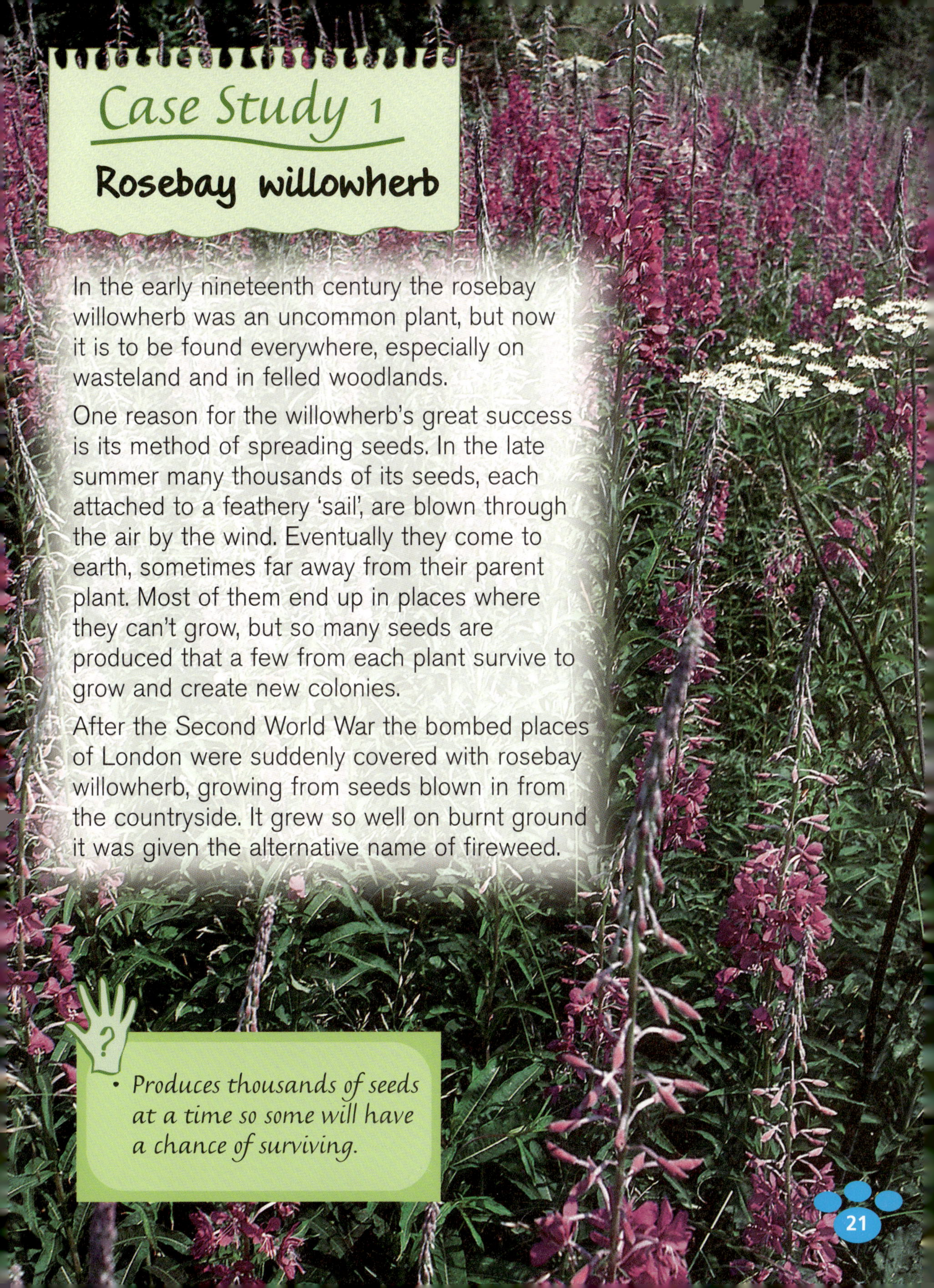

Case Study 1

Rosebay willowherb

In the early nineteenth century the rosebay willowherb was an uncommon plant, but now it is to be found everywhere, especially on wasteland and in felled woodlands.

One reason for the willowherb's great success is its method of spreading seeds. In the late summer many thousands of its seeds, each attached to a feathery 'sail', are blown through the air by the wind. Eventually they come to earth, sometimes far away from their parent plant. Most of them end up in places where they can't grow, but so many seeds are produced that a few from each plant survive to grow and create new colonies.

After the Second World War the bombed places of London were suddenly covered with rosebay willowherb, growing from seeds blown in from the countryside. It grew so well on burnt ground it was given the alternative name of fireweed.

- *Produces thousands of seeds at a time so some will have a chance of surviving.*

Case Study 2

Cuckoos

The cuckoo arrives in Britain from Africa in April, but unlike other **migrating** birds, it does not start nest building. Once other birds have built their nests and started to lay eggs, the cuckoo lays its own egg in their nest. The cuckoo is even able to adapt the colour and size of its egg to match the eggs of the **host species**.

The 'foster parent' birds do not realise that they have been tricked, and continue to feed the baby cuckoo, even though it may be much bigger than they are!

Cuckoo chick being fed by foster parent

- *Can disguise their eggs so they are the same shape and size as host eggs.*
- *Foster parents look after the cuckoo chicks until they are able to fly.*

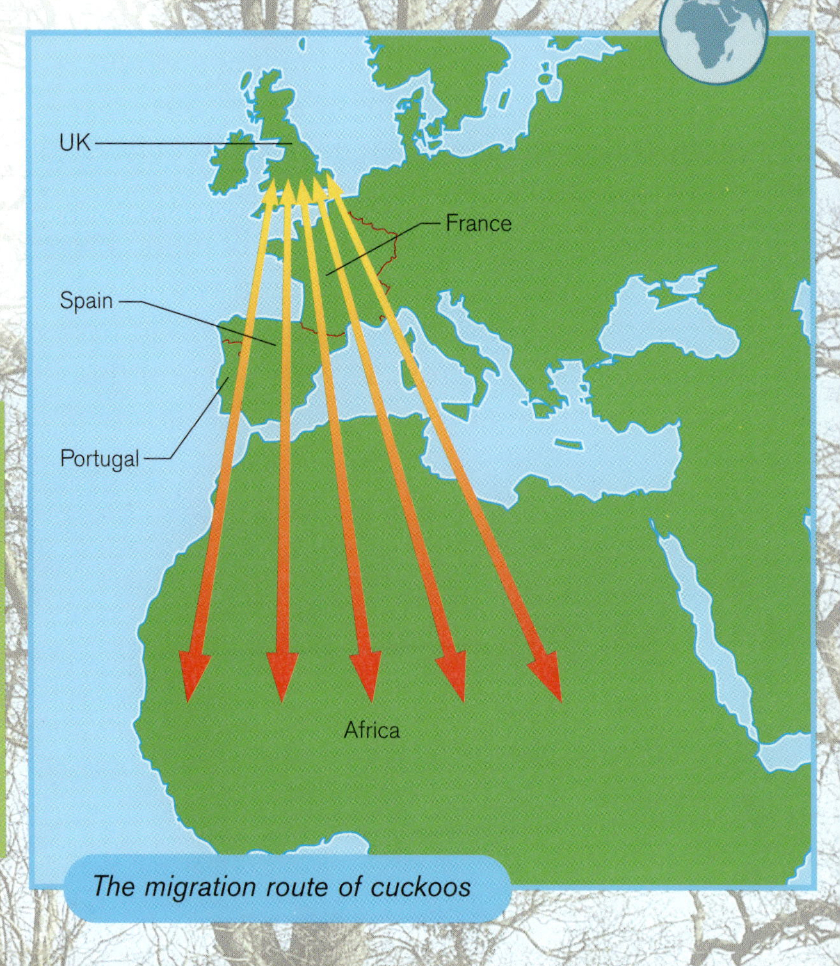

The migration route of cuckoos

Once they are hatched, the cuckoo chicks have another trick to make sure they survive. They have a sensitive patch on their backs, and if they feel something rubbing against it, they push hard to get rid of the irritating tickle – so they push the other chicks out of the nest!

The young cuckoos leave the nests in August and September, when they are able to fly back to Africa with no guidance from their parents.

Surviving the seasons

The changing seasons are a major challenge to wildlife. How do animals and plants cope as their food runs out? In summer and autumn there is warmth and plenty of food, but when winter comes the warmth and food disappear.

Storage of food for the winter and **hibernation** are the solution for some creatures; others, such as birds which are able to travel long distances, choose to migrate to warmer places.

Annual plants survive as seeds buried safe in the ground; **perennial** plants need other ways to live through the winter. **Deciduous** trees lose their leaves, while other plants develop methods to prevent themselves from freezing. Some borrow a trick from animals – they hibernate underground!

Pets such as tortoises hibernate over the winter months.

Case Study 1

Daffodils

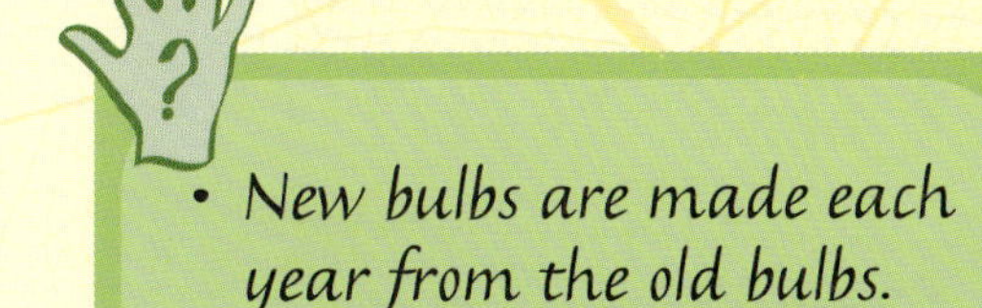

- *New bulbs are made each year from the old bulbs.*
- *Growing in the spring gives them more light, before the leaves of trees make shade.*

Spring flowers like the daffodil take advantage of the time before the leaves of trees block out the sunlight. During this period they are very busy, producing plenty of green leaves to make food, and flower stalks to produce seeds.

There is plenty going on below ground as well. The daffodil leaves and flowers grow from an underground bulb or food store. As the old bulb gives up its food to build the plant, new bulbs are being made ready for next year's plants. The bulbs are not just a food store, but a way of creating new daffodil plants, because each bulb made will be a separate plant, ready to grow as soon as the winter is over. A daffodil bulb can grow and produce a flower without any soil at all – try growing one in a bulb vase and watch the roots reaching down to the water.

Case Study 2

Dormice

In the autumn the dormouse feeds constantly, especially on hazelnuts, which are its favourite food. The dormouse needs to build up the stores of fat in its body if it is to survive hibernation.

For a dormouse, hibernation can be very long – some animals have even been known to sleep for nine months at a time.

As soon as the colder weather arrives in October, the dormouse prepares its sleeping quarters. It usually sleeps on the ground, rolled tightly into a ball in a nest of leaves and grass. Gradually, its body temperature and heart rate are lowered. The dormouse feels cold to the touch. Dormice usually sleep until the warmer weather of March or April. The life span of a dormouse is five years. This is a very long time for a creature of this size – they survive because they sleep so much!

- *Eats constantly in the autumn and stores up body fat.*
- *Sleeps for six months of the year or more!*

Changing habitats

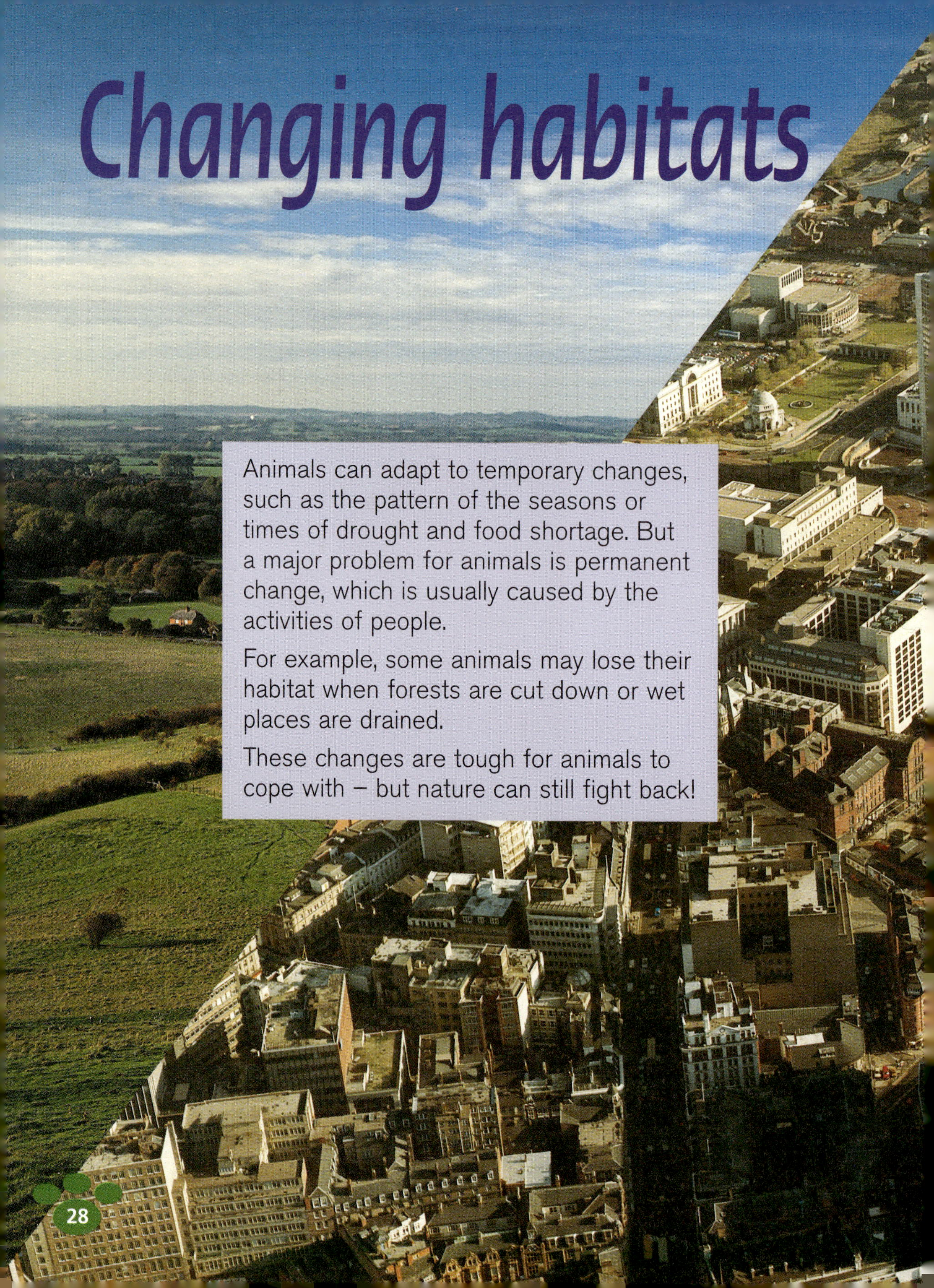

Animals can adapt to temporary changes, such as the pattern of the seasons or times of drought and food shortage. But a major problem for animals is permanent change, which is usually caused by the activities of people.

For example, some animals may lose their habitat when forests are cut down or wet places are drained.

These changes are tough for animals to cope with – but nature can still fight back!

Case Study 1

Urban foxes

The fox was once a country animal. When changes to the countryside made life difficult for foxes, they found new places to live and breed – in the city!

Urban foxes are born in March in an **earth** which might be in a town park or garden, or alongside a railway line. The first few weeks are dangerous times as the cubs are blind and helpless. But by October the young foxes will be big enough to find their own territory.

In some ways the city is an ideal habitat for the growing fox because there is plenty of food all the year round. Even foxes born late in the year can survive through the winter since food does not run out in the city as it does in the countryside.

This adaptable animal has found a new answer to the problem of survival in a changing world.

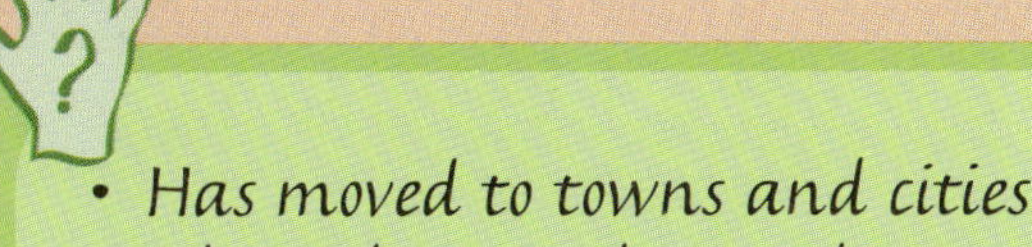

- *Has moved to towns and cities where there is always plenty of food.*

Case Study 2

Peppered moths

In the nineteenth century many parts of Britain were affected by air pollution. In these places surfaces were darkened by soot. This was bad news for light coloured insects – it was easier for birds to see them against the dark surface!

The peppered moth is unusual because it comes in two varieties. One is grey and speckled and the other nearly black. Before there was serious pollution, the speckled form was the most common, as it was camouflaged against the grey lichen that grew on tree trunks. Once the environment changed, the black variety became much more common, since this type had a much better chance of survival.

These days pollution, especially smoke, is much less of a problem and the population of peppered moths is changing again. Even in industrial areas the speckled peppered moth is on the increase.

- *The type with the best camouflage for the environment increases in numbers.*

Glossary

alga a simple type of plant, for example seaweed

annual a plant that lasts for only one year

bioluminescence production of light by living things

camouflage blending into the background

colony large group of animals of one species

deciduous a plant or animal which regularly sheds part of itself, eg. leaves, antlers

drought period of little or no rainfall

earth a fox's home

food chain series of creatures each dependent on the next as a source of food

fungus a type of plant that cannot make its own food, such as a mushroom

habitat place where an animal or plant lives

hibernation the ability of some animals to sleep through times when food is scarce

host species a species that provides a home or food for another species

insulate prevent heat or cold passing through

kidney part of the body that removes waste matter from the blood

maternity den a place prepared by an animal to give birth in

migration regular seasonal movement of animals

offspring young animals

perennial a plant that can live for a number of years

photosynthesis the process of turning air and water into food in green plants

predator a species that hunts and eats other species

prey a species hunted and eaten by another species

resource available supply

self sufficient able to supply one's own needs

species a particular kind of animal or plant

urban to do with towns and cities

water pressure weight of water pressing in on all sides

Index